Bodrum Travel Guide 2024

A Journey Beyond the Surface – Discover Hidden Stories, Local Delights, and Unforgettable Adventures in this Coastal Haven

Emily Catlett

EMILY CATLETT

EMILY CATLETT

MAP OF BODRUM

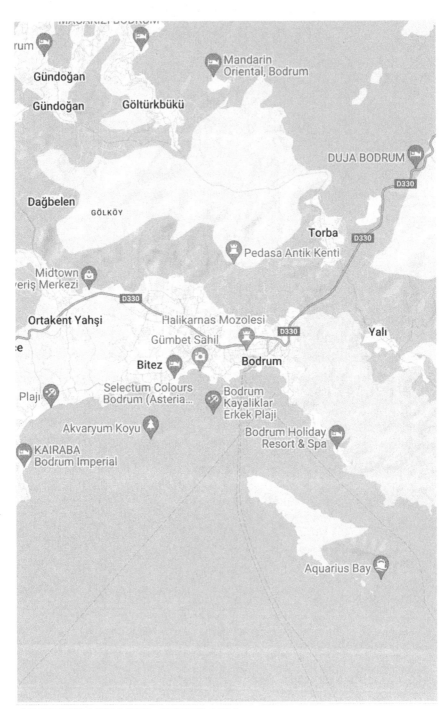

EMILY CATLETT

5 BODRUM TRAVEL GUIDE 2024

EMILY CATLETT

EMILY CATLETT

TABLE OF CONTENTS

EMILY CATLETT

10 BODRUM TRAVEL GUIDE 2024

INTRODUCTION

In the turquoise embrace of the Aegean Sea, where the sun-drenched coasts meet the whispers of ancient civilizations, sits a treasure of the Turkish Riviera Bodrum. As a dedicated traveller, I have wandered the world's corners, seeking narratives weaved in cobblestone alleyways and written in the colours of local marketplaces. Yet, it was the magical appeal of Bodrum that captivated my heart, calling me to explore its rich tapestry of history, culture, and untamed beauty.

Picture yourself wandering through the small streets of Bodrum's ancient town, where bougainvillaea pours over whitewashed buildings and the perfume of olive trees mingles with the sea wind. Feel the warmth of the sun on your cheeks as you travel the labyrinthine alleyways, each turn exposing hidden gems - from artisan workshops to quiet cafés booming with laughter.

In the pages that follow, I ask you to go on a trip with me, a seasoned traveller turned storyteller, as I unveil the mysteries of Bodrum. This book is more than simply a collection of practical ideas; it is a tale woven from personal interactions, provided with the goal of converting your stay into an amazing voyage.

From the famous silhouette of the Bodrum Castle standing watch over the bay to the lively anarchy of the Bodrum Bazaar, every chapter of this book is a window into the essence of this coastal paradise. Discover quiet coves where turquoise seas dance with the sun and ancient ruins echo stories of civilizations long gone. Whether you are an adventurous explorer, a history enthusiast, or a seeker of quiet moments, Bodrum has a narrative waiting for you.

So, let the pages of this book be your compass, directing you through the mosaic of Bodrum's delights. May it encourage you to taste the delicacies of local food, embrace the warmth of Turkish hospitality, and create memories that stay long after the voyage ends? Welcome to Bodrum - where every cobblestone tells a tale, and every sunset paints a masterpiece in the sky.

HISTORY OF BODRUM

Ancient Halicarnassus: Birthplace of Herodotus

Bodrum's history may be traced back to ancient times when it was known as Halicarnassus. The city achieved popularity in the 5th century BCE as the birthplace of the "Father of History," Herodotus. The Mausoleum at Halicarnassus, one of the Seven Wonders of the Ancient World, was created in the 4th century BCE in honour of Mausolus, a satrap of the Persian Empire. The Mausoleum's ruins remain a witness to the city's magnificence during this era.

Hellenistic and Roman Periods: The Influence of Alexander the Great

During the Hellenistic period, Bodrum fell under the influence of Alexander the Great, who conquered the province in the 4th century BCE. The city continued to prosper under Hellenistic administration, and its strategic position gave it a magnet for commerce and cultural interaction.

Under Roman authority, Bodrum further thrived, and significant constructions like the Roman Theater and the Myndos Gate were created. These ruins give insights into the architectural brilliance and urban planning of the period.

Byzantine and Ottoman Eras: Shifting Powers

As the Roman Empire crumbled, Bodrum underwent a number of changes in rulership. The Byzantines acquired power in the 7th century CE, leaving their imprint on the city with the building of the Bodrum Castle (also known as the Castle of St. Peter) in the early 15th century. This medieval stronghold, subsequently enlarged by the Knights of St. John, serves as a symbol of Bodrum's strategic importance.

In the 16th century, the Ottoman Empire, commanded by Suleiman the Magnificent, seized Bodrum. The city's status as a nautical hub continued to expand throughout the Ottoman administration, with the castle playing an important role in defending against pirate raids.

Modern Era: Transformation into a Cosmopolitan Destination

Bodrum saw substantial changes in the 20th century as it evolved from a sleepy fishing hamlet to a busy tourist attraction. The city's beautiful combination of historical charm and modern attractions attracts tourists from around the globe.

The Bodrum Museum of Underwater Archaeology, situated inside the Bodrum Castle, shows an outstanding collection of items collected from shipwrecks in the Aegean Sea, affording a unique view into the region's nautical past.

Contemporary Bodrum: A Mediterranean Gem

Today, Bodrum exists as a tribute to its complex history. Visitors may explore ancient ruins, meander through attractive towns, and relax on lovely beaches. The city's dynamic nightlife, premium resorts, and busy marketplaces add to its prominence as a sought-after destination.

EMILY CATLETT

WHY VISIT BODRUM IN 2024

1. Commendorating Bodrum's 100th Anniversary: In 2024, Bodrum will be commemorating its 100th anniversary since it was designated an autonomous district. This milestone will be honoured with spectacular events, festivals, and cultural displays that will provide visitors with a unique glimpse into Bodrum's rich history and traditions. It will be a great opportunity to discover and experience the local traditions, customs, and lifestyle, making your vacation to Bodrum even more unforgettable.

2. Moderate Weather: Bodrum is recognized for its Mediterranean environment, which means it gets long, hot summers and moderate winters. In 2024, the weather is forecast to be exceptionally moderate and pleasant, making it a perfect time to visit. The mild weather will enable you to enjoy outdoor activities, explore the town on foot, and bask in the sun at the lovely beaches without worrying about the blazing heat or freezing winds.

3. Less Crowded: Bodrum is a major tourist destination, bringing travellers from all over the globe. While this adds to the town's dynamic vibe, it may also result in crowded beaches, lengthy waits, and difficulties in locating housing. However, this won't be the case until 2024. With the worldwide pandemic causing a fall in tourism in recent years, 2024 is predicted to witness a steady rebound in

tourists, giving it a comparatively less crowded and more quiet period to explore Bodrum.

4. Exploring Historic Sites: Bodrum is home to numerous notable historical sites that date back to ancient times. One of the greatest attractions is the Bodrum Castle, built in 1402 by the Knights of Saint John. In 2024, the castle is anticipated to undergo repairs and upgrades, providing tourists a chance to experience it at its greatest. Additionally, a visit to the ancient city of Halicarnassus, home to the world-renowned Mausoleum of Halicarnassus, is a must-see for history aficionados.

5. Festivals and Events: Bodrum is renowned for its festivities, and 2024 is predicted to be a year full of festivals and events. From music and dance festivals to cultural exhibits and cuisine markets, there will be something for everyone. The Bodrum International Ballet Festival is a prominent event that promotes local and international ballet performances, while the Bodrum Jazz Festival draws jazz aficionados from all over the globe.

6. Premium Accommodations: With the booming tourist business in Bodrum, the town has experienced a surge in premium hotel alternatives. 2024 will be a perfect opportunity to see these magnificent hotels and resorts at their finest.

CHAPTER 1

GETTING TO BODRUM

TRANSPORTATION OPTIONS

Public Transportation

Dolmuş: These shared minibuses are the cheapest method to go about Bodrum and the surrounding region. They operate on predetermined routes and may be flagged down anytime along the road. Just let the driver know where you're heading and climb on! A journey from Bodrum to Gumbet will cost roughly 5₺.

Buses: There are also frequent buses that travel between Bodrum and other towns in the vicinity, such as Milas and Didim. These are a wonderful alternative if you're planning to visit farther away.

Boats: Bodrum is a renowned yachting location; therefore, there are lots of boats available for lease. This is a terrific opportunity to observe the coastline and visit the adjacent islands. You may also take a ferry from Bodrum to Kos, Greece.

Taxis

Taxis are frequently accessible in Bodrum and are a handy method to get about, particularly if you're going with baggage or at night. However, they may be pricey, so be careful to agree on a fee before you get in.

Car Rental

Renting a vehicle is a wonderful alternative if you want to explore the Bodrum Peninsula at your own leisure. There are various vehicle rental businesses in Bodrum, and you may pick up your car at the airport or in town. Just be careful to add in the expense of parking, which may be pricey in certain regions.

Walking and Cycling

Bodrum is a rather tiny town, so it's simple to get about on foot or by bicycle. This is a terrific way to view the sites and soak up the ambience. There are also lots of bike rental outlets in town.

AIRPORTS AND AIRLINES

Flying into Bodrum:

Milas-Bodrum Airport (BJV): The major entrance to Bodrum, situated around 35 kilometres southeast of the town centre. It serves various foreign and local airlines, particularly during high season. Expect direct flights from key European cities and seasonal connections from farther afield.

Dalaman Airport (DLM): A major airport around 120 km northwest of Bodrum. It provides additional travel alternatives, notably from the UK and Ireland, making it a suitable alternative, especially during high season when Milas-Bodrum Airport becomes congested. Be prepared for a lengthy transfer to Bodrum, however.

EMILY CATLETT

Airlines to Consider:

Turkish Airlines: The national airline provides extensive connections to Bodrum from many places worldwide, typically with simple one-stop layovers in Istanbul.

Pegasus Airlines: A budget-friendly choice with a solid network of European connections to Bodrum.

SunExpress: A joint venture between Turkish Airlines and Lufthansa, operating seasonal flights from key European cities.

Onur Air: A tiny Turkish airline offering direct flights from various European locations.

Charter Airlines: Several charter airlines provide seasonal flights to Bodrum, primarily from package vacation locations.

Tips for Booking Your Flight:

Book early: Especially during peak season (June-August), flights to Bodrum fill up rapidly. Book early in advance for the greatest discounts and flight alternatives.

Consider connecting flights: Depending on your origin, connecting flights via large hubs like Istanbul or Dubai can provide better costs and schedules.

Compare prices: Use flight comparison websites to check costs and discounts across multiple airlines and travel brokers.

Be flexible with dates: If feasible, go during shoulder seasons (May-June or September-October) for cheaper airfares and fewer people.

Check visa requirements: Ensure you have the relevant visa for Turkey before booking your journey.

Transfers from the Airport:

Taxis: These are widely accessible at both airports, allowing easy but costly journeys to Bodrum. Negotiate fares upfront for a reasonable price.

Shuttles: Shared shuttle busses run from the airports to different hotels and resorts in Bodrum, a budget-friendly choice but with lengthier journey durations.

Pre-booked transfers: Arrange a private transfer with your hotel or a local transportation operator for a hassle-free arrival.

PUBLIC TRANSPORTATION

The Dolmuş

The indisputable monarch of Bodrum's public transit is the dolmuş. These minibuses, emblazoned with their destinations painted on the front windshield, are your ticket to explore the Bodrum peninsula and beyond. Think of them as a hybrid between a bus and a shared cab, darting through congested streets and stopping wherever you indicate.

Riding the Dolmuş:

Finding your dolmuş: Head to the main dolmuş station near the Bodrum Otogar bus terminal. Smaller dolmuş kiosks are distributed around the city, generally near prominent sites or squares. Don't hesitate to ask nice locals for instructions.

Hopping on: Simply wave down a dolmuş headed to your selected destination. The driver will stop if there's room.

Paying your fare: Pay the driver straight upon boarding. Fares are very low, generally under 1.5 TRY for any distance inside the peninsula. Carry modest changes, as bigger notes may not be easily accepted.

Disembarking: Inform the driver where you want to get off by shouting "durak" (halt) or hitting the buzzer button.

Dolmuş Routes:

A huge network of dolmuş lines traverses the Bodrum peninsula, linking the city centre with major resorts, towns, and historical monuments.

These are a few of the busiest routes:

Bodrum to Turgutreis: This route operates every 10-15 minutes, great for beach hopping or seeing the vibrant resort town of Turgutreis.

Bodrum - Yalıkavak: This picturesque road takes you past magnificent coves and sumptuous beaches, culminating at the lovely fishing hamlet of Yalıkavak.

Bodrum - Gümüşlük: Journey through olive orchards and medieval villages to reach the laid-back paradise of Gümüşlük, noted for its natural mud spas and spectacular sunsets.

Bodrum to Milas: For further travel to other Turkish locations, get on a dolmuş to Milas, where the Bodrum International Airport is situated.

CHAPTER 2

ACCOMMODATION OPTIONS

HOTELS AND RESORTS

1. Mandarin Oriental, Bodrum

Located in the scenic Paradise Bay, Mandarin Oriental Bodrum is a magnificent resort that provides stunning views of the Aegean Sea. The resort has large rooms and suites, each with its own balcony or patio facing the sea. The resort also has five swimming pools, a private beach, a spa, and five restaurants serving a range of cuisines. The resort's design perfectly integrates contemporary and traditional Turkish features, providing a distinctive and opulent ambience. With exceptional service and top-notch facilities, Mandarin Oriental Bodrum is a great option for guests seeking a luxury and unforgettable stay in Bodrum.

2. Amanruya Bodrum

Nestled in a magnificent pine forest and facing the shimmering Aegean Sea, Amanruya Bodrum is a calm and private paradise. The resort provides magnificent stand-alone cabins with private pools, patios, and spectacular sea views. The style of this resort takes influence from traditional Turkish architecture, with stone walls, wooden beams, and tiled roofs. Amanruya Bodrum also provides a number of activities, including water sports, mountain biking, and cookery workshops. The resort's quiet setting, customized service, and opulent facilities make it a popular option for guests searching for a peaceful and elegant escape.

3. Kempinski Hotel Barbaros Bay Bodrum

Perched on a hilltop overlooking the enchanting Barbaros Bay, Kempinski Hotel Barbaros Bay Bodrum is a gorgeous 5-star resort that provides a perfect combination of luxury and seclusion. The resort has exquisite rooms and suites, each with its own balcony or patio, affording spectacular sea views. The resort also has an outstanding selection of services, including a private beach, a spa, a fitness centre, and five restaurants offering great Turkish and international cuisine. With its exceptional location, opulent facilities, and top-notch service, Kempinski Hotel Barbaros Bay Bodrum is a popular option for guests seeking a sumptuous and unforgettable stay in Bodrum.

4. Jumeirah Bodrum Palace

Set on a secluded peninsula on the Bodrum coast, Jumeirah Bodrum Palace is a magnificent beachfront resort that provides breathtaking views of the Aegean Sea. The resort's design is influenced by Ottoman architecture, with magnificent domes, arches, and minarets. The resort has big and opulent accommodations, each with its own patio or balcony and some with its own private pools. With its magnificent beach, four swimming pools, spa, and eight restaurants, Jumeirah Bodrum Palace provides a broad selection of activities and services for guests to enjoy. The resort's luxury atmosphere, great service, and gorgeous location make it a popular option for guests seeking a sumptuous and indulgent stay in Bodrum.

5. Caresse Resort & Spa, a Luxury Collection Property

Situated on a beautiful peninsula, Caresse, a Luxury Collection Resort and spa, features spectacular views of the Aegean Sea and Bodrum Castle. The resort is only a few minutes away from the busy town centre, making it an excellent site for tourists who wish to experience the town's nightlife while enjoying a tranquil and elegant stay. The resort has beautiful rooms and suites, each with its own balcony or patio, affording stunning sea views. The resort also includes a private beach, a spa, and three restaurants providing a range of cuisines. With its excellent location, sumptuous facilities, and personalized service, Caresse, a Luxury Collection Resort and spa, is a great option for tourists seeking a blend of luxury and convenience in Bodrum.

VACATION RENTALS

1. Villa Alesta

Situated in the picturesque town of Yalikavak, Villa Alesta provides a luxurious and unique holiday experience. This lovely property features five large bedrooms, all with en-suite bathrooms, and can sleep up to 10 people. The interior is stylishly designed with modern furniture and offers a fully equipped kitchen, an open-plan living space with stunning sea views, and a private infinity pool. With close access to the beach and local facilities, this vacation rental is excellent for families or groups of friends searching for a calm but accessible setting.

2. Bodrum Loft

If you're seeking more contemporary and stylish lodging, Bodrum Loft is the best option. Located in the centre of Bodrum, this contemporary loft apartment provides a unique and pleasant stay for up to 4 people. The inside is elegantly designed with a combination of minimalist and industrial features, and the big floor-to-ceiling windows allow lots of natural light and great views of the city. Guests may also enjoy the rooftop patio with a private hot tub and amazing views of Bodrum Castle.

3. Aegean Dreams

Situated in the scenic hamlet of Gumusluk, Aegean Dreams is a quaint and traditional holiday property that emanates the right blend of comfort and authenticity. This 3-bedroom property boasts gorgeous stone walls, wooden ceilings, and a huge living space with a comfortable fireplace. The outside area offers a private pool, a verdant garden with a BBQ, and breathtaking views of the Aegean Sea. It's the perfect refuge for people seeking a tranquil and lovely stay in Bodrum.

4. Villa Serenity

For a genuinely magnificent and sumptuous holiday experience, Villa Serenity is the best option. Located in the upscale area of Turkbuku, this 6-bedroom home provides a calm and secluded location with amazing sea views. The inside is designed with luxury furniture and facilities, including a fully equipped kitchen, a home theatre, and a private spa with a sauna and Turkish bath. Outside, visitors may relax in the infinity pool or enjoy a meal in the al fresco dining area, which is equipped with a built-in BBQ.

5. Sunset Beach House

Last but not least, the Sunset Beach House is a wonderful holiday property located on a secluded length of beach in the picturesque hamlet of Gundogan. This huge 4-bedroom home offers a modern design with big windows, providing natural light and magnificent sea views. The outside space is excellent for sunbathing and eating under the stars, and visitors can also take a plunge in the heated infinity pool or chill in the Jacuzzi. With its exceptional position and exquisite facilities, Sunset Beach House provides a genuinely memorable vacation experience.

CAMPING AND GLAMPING OPTIONS

1. Kefaluka Resort Camping

Located in Akyarlar, Kefaluka Resort Camping provides a luxury and upmarket camping experience. The resort features a magnificent beachside setting with amazing views of the Aegean Sea. The campground includes a range of lodging choices, including tents, cabins, and RVs, all furnished with contemporary conveniences, including comfy mattresses, private toilets, and air conditioning. Guests may also enjoy the resort's various amenities, such as a swimming pool, restaurant, and bar. Kefaluka Resort Camping is an excellent option for guests searching for a combination of nature and luxury.

2. Eskiçeşme Glamping

Eskiçeşme Glamping is situated on the outskirts of Bodrum and provides a unique and genuine experience for glampers. The campsite is nestled in a magnificent orchard and provides a number of housing options, including elegant tents, tree huts, and traditional Bodrum-style cottages. Guests may also join in numerous activities such as horseback riding, yoga, and culinary lessons. With its historic Turkish environment, Eskiçeşme Glamping is a terrific alternative for those wanting an intensive cultural experience.

3. Letoonia Club & Hotel Glamping

Letoonia Club & Hotel is located in a private cove in Fethiye, just a short boat trip from Bodrum. This all-inclusive resort also provides a glamping option that is excellent for families and parties. The campsite includes beautiful and comfy tents equipped with all basic conveniences. Guests may also enjoy a selection of activities such as swimming, water sports, and nightly entertainment events. Letoonia Club & Hotel Glamping is an ideal alternative for vacationers searching for a blend of adventure and comfort.

4. Sign by Ersan Glamping

Located on a secluded peninsula, Sign by Ersan Glamping provides a unique and personal glamping experience. The campsite is surrounded by beautiful nature and provides elegant tented Accommodation with a private pool, Jacuzzi, and outdoor shower. Guests may enjoy the resort's various amenities, including a spa, fitness centre, and restaurants. With its tranquil and private position, Sign by Ersan Glamping is excellent for honeymooners and couples searching for a romantic holiday in Bodrum.

5. Bodrum Camping International

Bodrum Camping International is a budget-friendly and family-friendly camping alternative situated within a short walk from Bodrum's city centre. The campground provides numerous lodging alternatives, such as tents, bungalows, and mobile homes. Guests may also enjoy the campsite's own beach, swimming pool, and restaurant. The closeness to the city centre makes this campground a good alternative for those wishing to enjoy the bustling city of Bodrum.

CHAPTER 3

ATTRACTIONS AND LANDMARKS

BODRUM CASTLE

Getting There:

Bodrum is well-connected to major cities in Turkey and Europe. Milas-Bodrum Airport acts as the major gateway for air passengers, providing flights from numerous foreign and domestic places. Once in Bodrum, the castle is readily accessible by vehicle, taxi, or public transit.

History of Bodrum Castle:

Built between 1402 and 1437 by the Knights Hospitaller, Bodrum Castle functioned as a fortification during the Crusades. The castle changed hands multiple times throughout the ages, seeing the impact of the Ottoman Empire and the Republic of Turkey. Today, visitors may study the castle's history via its well-preserved architecture and intriguing exhibitions.

Highlights & Must-See Attractions:

The Castle Grounds:

Begin your adventure by visiting the castle's enormous grounds, encircled by majestic walls and turrets.

Take in panoramic views of the Bodrum Peninsula and the Aegean Sea from key vantage points.

The English Tower:

Visit the English Tower, one of the castle's principal towers, which houses the Museum of Underwater Archaeology.

Discover a fascinating collection of relics rescued from shipwrecks, highlighting Bodrum's rich nautical heritage.

The French Tower:

Explore the French Tower, home to the Museum of Underwater Archaeology's second display, exhibiting remnants from historic shipwrecks.

The German Tower:

The German Tower includes the magnificent Glass Shipwreck Hall, showing well-preserved shipwrecks and their contents.

The Topkapi Tower:

Climb to the Topkapi Tower for amazing views over Bodrum and the surrounding environs.

Learn about the castle's history as a military fortification and its architectural importance.

EMILY CATLETT

The Chapel of St. Peter:

Visit the castle's chapel, which is dedicated to St. Peter and embellished with medieval paintings and religious objects.

Practical Information:

Opening Hours:

Bodrum Castle is normally available to tourists from 9:00 AM to 7:00 PM. Check for any changes in schedule due to holidays or maintenance.

Admission Fees:

Entrance costs are modest, with reductions available for students and elderly.

Guided Tours:

Consider attending a guided tour to obtain deeper insights into the castle's history and importance.

Photography and Respect:

Photography is permitted in most locations; however, be courteous of signage denoting prohibited zones.

Wear comfortable attire and sturdy shoes for exploring the castle's numerous floors and terrains.

ANCIENT THEATER OF BODRUM

1: Historical Overview

1.1 Origins and Construction

The Ancient Theater of Bodrum, also known as the Bodrum Amphitheater, dates back to the Hellenistic era, established in the 4th century BCE. Initially, it functioned as a location for theatre performances and gladiator competitions.

1.2 Architectural Features

Explore the architectural grandeur of the theatre, which held roughly 13,000 people. Learn about its well-preserved construction, including the skene (stage building), orchestra, and cavea (seating area), showing a harmonic combination of Greek and Roman elements.

2: Significance in Ancient Times

2.1 Cultural Hub

Delve into the importance of the theatre as a cultural centre, where the residents of ancient Halicarnassus congregated for amusement, religious rites, and political events. Uncover the historical events that happened behind its walls.

2.2 Ongoing Archaeological Discoveries

Discuss current archaeological finds and continuing excavations that continue to unravel the mysteries of the Ancient Theater, giving insight into the life of the people who formerly inhabited the area.

3: Planning Your Visit in 2024

3.1 Accessibility

Provide data on how to reach Bodrum, including information on the Milas-Bodrum Airport, transit choices inside the town, and accessibility to nearby attractions.

3.2 Opening Hours and Admission

Inform readers about the operation hours of the Ancient Theater, entry rates, and any special events or exhibits that could overlap with their visit.

3.3 Guided Tours and Educational Programs

Highlight the availability of guided tours and educational programs that give in-depth insights into the history and architecture of the Ancient Theater. Include suggestions for reliable travel operators.

4: Exploring the Surrounding Area

4.1 Bodrum Museum of Underwater Archaeology

Encourage guests to prolong their historical adventure by touring the neighbouring Bodrum Museum of Underwater Archaeology, based in the Bodrum Castle, which shows objects from ancient shipwrecks.

4.2 Mausoleum at Halicarnassus

Suggest a visit to one of the Seven Wonders of the Ancient World, the Mausoleum at Halicarnassus, situated nearby. Provide insights about its history and relevance.

5: Practical Tips and Recommendations

5.1 Dress Code and Comfort

Advise guests on acceptable clothes for viewing historical places, including the environment and the necessity for comfortable Footwear.

5.2 Local Cuisine and Dining Options

Introduce readers to the local cuisine of Bodrum, offering neighbouring eateries where they may sample traditional Turkish delicacies after a day of sightseeing.

5.3 Responsible Tourism

Emphasize the significance of conserving the historical place and practising responsible tourist practices to maintain its integrity for future generations.

BODRUM MUSEUM OF UNDERWATER ARCHAEOLOGY

1. History of Bodrum Museum of Underwater Archaeology

1.1 The Castle of St. Peter

The museum is set inside the historic Castle of St. Peter, erected by the Knights of St. John in the 15th century. Over the years, the castle served numerous uses, including a military outpost and a jail. In 1962, the Turkish government renovated it into a museum, showing antiquities salvaged from shipwrecks in the Aegean area.

1.2 Foundation of the Museum

The Bodrum Museum of Underwater Archaeology was formally created in 1964 under the guidance of Turkish archaeologist and diver Dr. George Bass. The museum's principal emphasis is on underwater excavations and the preservation of marine archaeological artefacts.

2. Exhibits and Collections

2.1 Shipwreck Artifacts

The museum's major appeal is its enormous collection of items rescued from shipwrecks. Notable displays include relics from the Uluburun Shipwreck, going back to the Late Bronze Age, and the Gelidonya Shipwreck, showing the Late Bronze Age to the Early Iron Age transition.

2.2 Glass Hall

The Glass Hall features an amazing exhibit of glass antiquities, featuring delicate items such as bowls, bottles, and lamps. These pieces give insights into ancient glass-making skills and trading networks.

2.3 Amphora Hall

The Amphora Hall shows a broad assortment of amphorae, ancient jars used for carrying items like wine, olive oil, and grain. The collection covers many historical eras, depicting the growth of marine commerce in the Mediterranean.

2.4 Coin Collection

A substantial component of the museum is devoted to a massive coin collection. These coins, found in numerous shipwrecks, give an insight into the economic and trading activity of ancient civilizations.

3. Practical Information for Visitors

3.1 Opening Hours and Admission

The museum is normally available to tourists every day except Mondays.

It is essential to check the official website for the most up-to-date information on operating hours and entry rates.

3.2 Guided Tours

Guided tours are provided for guests wanting a more in-depth knowledge of the exhibits. Knowledgeable interpreters give historical background and tales, enriching the whole museum experience.

3.3 Location and Accessibility

Situated in the middle of Bodrum, the museum is readily accessible via public transit or on foot from several areas in the town. The Castle of St. Peter itself is a renowned landmark, making it simple to spot.

3.4 Nearby Attractions

Visitors may make the most of their stay by seeing additional sights in Bodrum, such as the Bodrum Amphitheater, the Mausoleum at Halicarnassus, and the Bodrum Maritime Museum.

MAUSOLEUM AT HALICARNASSUS

1. History and Significance:

1.1 Construction and Purpose: The Mausoleum was created by the Greek architects Satyros and Pythius and was meant to be a mausoleum for Mausolus, integrating many architectural styles, including Greek, Egyptian, and Lycian influences.

1.2 Destruction and Rediscovery: The Mausoleum existed for centuries until it was devastated by a succession of earthquakes in the Middle Ages. The remains were eventually repurposed by the Knights of St. John to create Bodrum Castle. Excavations in the 19th and 20th centuries unearthed the ruins of the Mausoleum, enabling its rebuilding in contemporary times.

2. Location and Accessibility:

2.1 Location: The Mausoleum is located in Bodrum, a gorgeous seaside town on the southwest coast of Turkey. It is conveniently accessible and a renowned attraction in the area.

2.2 Getting There:

By Air: The closest airport is Milas-Bodrum Airport, which is about 36 kilometres away. Taxis and rental vehicles are available to transport to Bodrum from the airport.

By Sea: Bodrum is accessible by ferry from different Greek islands, making it a handy stop for visitors touring the Aegean.

3. Visiting the Mausoleum:

3.1 Opening Hours and Entrance Fee: The site is normally open from early morning until early evening. It's essential to verify the current timetable before organizing your visit.

Entrance fees may apply, and there may be reductions for students and elderly.

3.2 Guided Tours: Consider attending a guided tour to obtain a fuller knowledge of the historical and architectural importance of the Mausoleum. Knowledgeable guides may give insights into the site's history and answer inquiries.

4. What to See and Do:

4.1 The Mausoleum Complex:

Explore the different components of the Mausoleum, including the enormous stairway, the colonnade, the pyramid, and the chariot sculptures. Admire the elaborate friezes and sculptures that formerly graced the building.

4.2 Bodrum Museum of Underwater Archaeology: Many relics from the Mausoleum are on show in the Bodrum Museum of Underwater Archaeology, situated within Bodrum Castle. Consider visiting the museum to view a selected selection of objects relating to the Mausoleum.

5. Practical Tips:

5.1 Dress Comfortably: Wear comfortable clothes and sturdy shoes since you will be touring archaeological archaeological remains.

5.2 Sun Protection: The location may be hot and sunny, so pack sunscreen, a hat, and lots of water.

5.3 Respect the Site: Follow the regulations and guidelines to protect the historical integrity of the Mausoleum. Avoid touching or climbing on the historic buildings.

EMILY CATLETT

BODRUM WINDMILLS

Bodrum: A Gateway to Ancient Beauty

1. Historical Overview

Bodrum has a history stretching back to ancient times, with its origins extending back to Halicarnassus, an old Greek city. The city's historical importance is reflected in its well-preserved remains, especially the Mausoleum at Halicarnassus, one of the Seven Wonders of the Ancient World.

2. Cultural Riches

Modern-day Bodrum perfectly mixes its ancient history with a thriving current culture. Visitors may visit the Bodrum Museum of Underwater Archaeology, situated in the Bodrum Castle, showing items from shipwrecks going back to antiquity.

Bodrum Windmills: A Glimpse into Tradition

1. Historical Significance

The Bodrum Windmills, commonly known as "Yel Değirmenleri," are a collection of antique windmills placed on the hills around the Bodrum Peninsula. Dating back to the 18th century, these windmills were formerly vital for grinding grains and supplying food to the surrounding inhabitants.

2. Architectural Marvels

The windmills, with their cylindrical stone constructions and conical tops, illustrate classic Ottoman architecture. Each windmill gives a panoramic view of the surrounding landscapes, making them not only practical constructions but also great vantage points for taking in the spectacular environment.

Exploring Bodrum Windmills

1. Location and Accessibility

The windmills are ideally positioned on the hills above Bodrum, allowing tourists a tranquil retreat from the hectic city below. Accessible by automobile or a picturesque stroll, the trip to the windmills is an experience in itself.

2. Sunset Splendor

For a really stunning experience, arrange your visit during the golden hour. The Bodrum Windmills give an exceptional vantage position to view the sun sinking over the Aegean Sea, throwing a warm light over the landscape and creating a captivating mood.

Practical Tips for Travelers

1. Best Time to Visit

While Bodrum is a year-round destination, the spring and fall months are perfect for great weather, fewer people, and beautiful

EMILY CATLETT

sceneries. Sunset excursions to the windmills are especially fascinating during these seasons.

2. Local Cuisine and Hospitality

Don't miss the chance to enjoy Bodrum's wonderful food, inspired by both Turkish and Mediterranean cuisines. Additionally, meeting with the welcoming people will lend a warm and personal touch to your trip experience.

BODRUM MARINA

1. History and Overview:

Bodrum Marina has a rich history, reaching back to ancient times. The city of Halicarnassus, which existed at the same site, was home to one of the Seven Wonders of the Ancient World - the Mausoleum at Halicarnassus. Today, the marina serves as a gateway for yachts and boats, and its dynamic environment draws visitors and residents alike.

2. Attractions:

a. Castle of St. Peter (Bodrum Castle):

Dominating the skyline, Bodrum Castle is a medieval stronghold erected by the Knights of St. John in the 15th century. It holds the Museum of Underwater Archaeology, showing objects from shipwrecks and prehistoric eras.

b. Mausoleum at Halicarnassus:

Although partially damaged, the Mausoleum's ruins and the antiquities unearthed from its location may be studied in the Bodrum Museum of Underwater Archaeology.

c. Bodrum Amphitheater:

Located a short distance away, the Bodrum Amphitheater provides breathtaking views of the city and the Aegean Sea. It's a well-preserved antique theatre with a capacity for 13,000 people.

3. Activities:

a. Boat Trips & Cruises:

Bodrum Marina is the best starting place for boat adventures and island cruises. Visitors may visit surrounding islands like Kos and Rhodes or go on a leisurely boat excursion along the Turkish shoreline.

b. Water Sports:

The marina provides chances for different water activities, including sailing, diving, and snorkelling. Adventurous guests may indulge in these activities against the background of Bodrum's gorgeous blue seas.

4. Dining and Nightlife:

a. Seafront Restaurants:

Indulge in Turkish and foreign cuisine at the several eateries around the waterfront. Fresh fish, classic mezes, and Turkish treats are widely available.

b. Cafés and Bars:

Enjoy a relaxed day or evening at the seaside cafés and pubs. Sip on Turkish tea or coffee while taking in the panoramic views, or enjoy Bodrum's dynamic nightlife at the different pubs and clubs.

5. Shopping: Bodrum Marina provides a mix of boutique boutiques, souvenir shops, and marketplaces. Visitors may discover handcrafted crafts, textiles, jewellery, and other unique goods that represent the local culture.

6. Practical Tips:

a. Best Time to Visit:

The summer months (May to September) bring mild weather and perfect conditions for outdoor activities. However, spring and autumn give a more suitable atmosphere for exploring.

b. Transportation:

Bodrum is accessible by air, with Milas-Bodrum Airport being the closest. Once in Bodrum, taxis, buses, and rental vehicles are widely accessible for mobility inside the city.

c. Accommodation:

There are many lodging alternatives, including luxury hotels, boutique guesthouses, and budget-friendly hostels, giving a variety of choices for varied tastes and budgets.

CHAPTER 4

BEACHES AND WATER ACTIVITIES

BODRUM PENINSULA BEACHES

For the Sun Worshipper:

Bitez Beach: This crescent-shaped jewel provides shallow seas, smooth sand, and a laidback ambience, excellent for families and anyone seeking quiet. Sunbeds and umbrellas surround the coastline, while watersports like kayaking and paddleboarding provide a touch of excitement.

Gümbet Beach: If you seek a dynamic atmosphere, Gümbet Beach is your home. Bustling with sunbathers, watersports enthusiasts, and beach bars, it pulsates with activity from dawn to dusk. Parasailing, jet skiing, and banana boat excursions are just a few ways to liven up your beach experience.

Kuum Beach: Nestled between Gümüşlük and Yalıkavak, Kuum Beach is a paradise for elegance and exclusivity. Beach clubs with infinity pools and luxurious loungers provide a piece of heaven, while the crystal-clear seas call for a refreshing plunge.

For the Adventurer:

Camel Beach: Accessible only by boat, Camel Beach is a remote haven. Its rough beauty, with cliffs surrounding the turquoise seas, is great for snorkelling, diving, and finding secret coves. Keep a watch out for the native wild camels that wander the neighbourhood.

Paradise Bay: This hidden treasure near Türkbükü is a sanctuary for windsurfers and kitesurfers. The powerful Aegean breezes offer the ideal arena for these adrenaline-pumping pursuits. Witness professional surfers cutting through the waves, or try your shot at catching the wind yourself.

Black Island: Take a boat journey to Karadağ, or Black Island, for a unique beach experience. Volcanic sand, hot springs pouring from the cliffs, and mud baths famed for their medicinal benefits make this a beach unlike any other.

For the History Buff:

Kumsandal Beach: This beach near Bodrum Castle provides a combination of sun, sand, and history. Soak in the sun on the golden sands, then visit the ancient ruins of the Mausoleum at Halicarnassus, one of the Seven Wonders of the Ancient World.

Ortakent Beach: This beach on Kos Island was previously a Greek fishing hamlet. Today, it's a pleasant place with tavernas selling fresh seafood and historical sights like the Myndos Gate, a gateway to ancient Caria.

WATERSPORTS AND DIVING

Watersports Galore:

Windsurfing and Kitesurfing: Bodrum's breezy coastlines and constant meltem breezes make it a windsurfer's and kitesurfer's delight. Numerous beaches, including Yahsi Ciftlik, Gumbet Bay, and Akyarlar, provide ideal conditions for novices and seasoned riders alike. Schools and rental businesses offer equipment and coaching, guaranteeing you catch the ideal wave.

Sailing & Catamaran Cruises: Glide over the turquoise waves on a sailboat or catamaran, taking in the beautiful sights of Bodrum's shoreline and adjacent Greek islands. Explore secret coves, quiet bays, and lovely fishing towns at your own speed. Several tour companies provide full-day and multi-day adventures, replete with snorkelling breaks and tasty aboard meals.

Scuba Diving and Snorkeling: Dive into the captivating underwater realm of the Aegean Sea. Bodrum provides a multitude of dive locations, from shallow reefs filled with colourful fish to shipwrecks and ancient ruins, providing historical interest. Diving facilities cater to all levels, including starting classes, guided dives, and equipment rentals. Even snorkelers may marvel at the underwater kaleidoscope from the surface.

Stand-Up Paddleboarding (SUP): Enjoy a calm tour of the shoreline on a SUP board. Paddle at your own speed, take up the sun, and find secret coves and inlets unreachable by land. SUP is a terrific sport for all ages and fitness levels, presenting a new view of Bodrum's beauties.

BOAT TOURS AND CRUISES

1. Types of Boat Tours:

 a. Daily Boat Tours: Ideal for tourists with limited time, these day-long excursions take you to famous places like Black Island, Camel Beach, and Aquarium Bay.

Enjoy swimming, snorkelling, and sunbathing while appreciating the stunning views of the Bodrum Peninsula.

b. Sunset Cruises: Experience the splendour of Bodrum's sunset over the Aegean Sea. Sunset cruises frequently include supper, offering a romantic mood for couples and a tranquil setting for lone visitors.

c. Private Yacht Charters: For a more customized experience, hire a private yacht. Tailor the route to your tastes, explore hidden beaches, and eat a personalized lunch served on board.

d. Gulet Cruises: Traditional wooden sailing boats, known as gulets, provide a unique opportunity to explore Bodrum's coastline. Multi-day gulet cruises give a leisurely voyage, mixing relaxation with cultural discovery.

2. Top Destinations:

a. Cleopatra Island: Famous for its beautiful golden sand, Cleopatra Island is a must-visit. Legend has it that Cleopatra imported the sand from Egypt, making it one of the most fascinating destinations on boat cruises.

b. Black Island (Kara Ada): Known for its hot springs, Black Island is a popular resort for people seeking relaxation. The warm, mineral-rich waters give a rejuvenating experience.

c. Rabbit Island (Tavsan Adasi): Explore the lovely Rabbit Island, named for the wild rabbits that inhabit it. The island is great for snorkelling and underwater exploring.

d. Orak Island: A tranquil place with crystal-clear seas, Orak Island is popular among snorkelers. The undersea habitat here is filled with colourful marine life.

3. Tips for a Memorable Boat Tour:

a. Choose the Right excursion: Consider your tastes and interests while picking a boat excursion. Whether you prefer leisure, adventure, or cultural discovery, there's a trip suited for you.

b. Pack Essentials:

Bring necessities like sunscreen, a hat, Swimwear, and a camera to record the gorgeous scenery. Some trips supply snorkelling gear, but it's recommended to check in advance.

c. Respect the Environment: Practice responsible tourism by respecting the maritime environment. Avoid trash, and observe standards for snorkelling and swimming to conserve the aquatic habitat.

d. Book in Advance: Especially during high tourist seasons, it's best to book your boat excursion in advance to reserve your seat and ensure a hassle-free experience.

CHAPTER 5

SHOPPING AND MARKETS

BODRUM BAZAAR

What to Buy at the Bodrum Bazaar

The Bodrum Bazaar is a heaven for shopping. Here are just a handful of the things you may find:

Traditional Turkish handicrafts: Carpets, rugs, kilims, jewellery, pottery, leather products, and hand-painted ceramics are all popular items.

Textiles: Silks, cotton, and linens in a range of colours and designs are great for picking up unique mementoes or presents.

Spices and herbs: Stock up on saffron, cumin, paprika, oregano, and other spices to give a bit of Turkish flavour to your food.

Food: Fresh fruits and veggies, olives, cheeses, nuts, and chocolates are all appealing pleasures to savour while you're shopping.

Souvenirs: Turkish coffee pots, nazar boncuğu (evil eye beads), and souvenirs with the Turkish flag are popular selections.

Tips for Haggling

Haggling is part of the enjoyment of shopping at the bazaar. Here are a few strategies to help you obtain the greatest deals:

Start with a modest offer: Don't be scared to offer half of the asking amount. The worst the vendor can say is no.

Be prepared to walk away: If you don't like the price, be prepared to walk away. The seller may come down if they fear they're about to lose a deal.

Be nice and respectful: A little grin and nice talk may go a long way in securing a decent bargain.

Where to Eat in the Bodrum Bazaar

After all that shopping, you're likely to be hungry. Here are a few wonderful places to dine in the bazaar:

Lokantasi: These modest, family-run eateries provide typical Turkish home food.

Pide: Turkish flatbreads topped with meat, veggies, or cheese are a great and economical alternative.

Gözleme: Savory pancakes stuffed with potatoes, cheese, or spinach are a popular street dish.

Dolma: Stuffed grape leaves, peppers, or eggplant are a popular Turkish delicacy.

Baklava: Flaky pastry stuffed with nuts and honey is a must-try delicious delight.

Opening Hours

The Bodrum Bazaar is open every day from 9:00 am until 10:00 pm. However, some vendors may shut for lunch or nap in the early afternoon.

Getting There

The Bodrum Bazaar is situated in the middle of Bodrum town, only a short walk from the harbour. You may also take a dolmuş (local minibus) or cab.

Tips for Your Visit

Wear comfortable shoes, since you'll be doing a lot of walking.

Bring cash since not all booths take credit cards.

Be prepared for crowds, particularly during the summer months.

Don't be scared to get lost! The best way to enjoy the bazaar is to roam around and investigate.

LOCAL MARKETS

Bodrum Farmers' Market:

What's on offer: Dive into a kaleidoscope of colours and smells at the Bodrum Farmers' Market. Every Tuesday and Friday, local farmers assemble to present their finest crop. From sun-ripened tomatoes and jewel-toned eggplants to plump olives and crusty loaves of bread, this market is a heaven for foodies. Don't miss the booths loaded with aromatic spices, honey oozing from wooden barrels, and heaps of delicious apricots and figs.

Tips: Come early for the finest variety, and be prepared to haggle good-naturedly. Cash is king here, so come loaded with Turkish lira. Wear comfortable shoes and bring your reusable bags to transport your loot.

Bodrum Municipality Bazaar:

What's on offer: Step back in time at the Bodrum Municipality Bazaar, a convoluted maze of covered booths brimming with treasures? Carpets in a riot of hues adorn the ground, while handwoven fabrics, shining copperware, and elaborately painted ceramics vie for space on shelves. Be sure to check out the kiosks decked with leather purses, silver jewellery, and hand-painted evil eye trinkets – excellent for unique gifts.

Tips: Haggling is expected here, so don't be bashful about making an offer. Take your time to explore and compare costs before committing to a purchase. Cash is recommended; however, some booths could take credit cards. There will be a lot of walking, so wear comfortable shoes.

Bodrum Bar Street Market:

What's on offer: As the sun slips below the horizon, the Bodrum Bar Street Market comes alive with a kaleidoscope of sights and sounds. Fairy lights glimmer above, providing a lovely glow on vendors offering handcrafted jewellery, odd trinkets, and local artesanato. Live music overflows from surrounding pubs, contributing to the lively mood. Fuel your shopping binge with gözleme (savoury Turkish pancakes) or drink freshly squeezed fruit juices while you peruse.

Tips:

The market becomes bustling in the evenings, so come after supper for the greatest experience. Be prepared for crowds, particularly on weekends. Cash is vital since most vendors are modest and family-run. Wear comfortable shoes and dress for the weather, since the nights might be chilly.

SOUVENIRS AND TRADITIONAL CRAFTS

Textiles and Carpets:

Kilims: These flat woven tapestries are a mainstay of Turkish handcraft, and Bodrum's kilims are known for their brilliant colours and complicated geometric designs. They make fantastic wall hangings, tablecloths, or even picnic blankets.

Handwoven carpets: Carpets are another favourite gift from Bodrum, and you'll find a broad selection of types and sizes to pick from, from classic Oushak rugs with their floral themes to contemporary kilim-inspired designs.

Jewelry:

Evil eye: The evil eye, or Nazar back, is a popular protective symbol in Turkey, and you'll find it decorating everything from jewellery to home décor. Bodrum's evil eye jewellery is especially stunning, with exquisite silver settings and bright beads.

Gold and silver jewellery: Bodrum's gold and silver jewellery is noted for its exquisite workmanship and timeless designs. You'll discover everything from classic Ottoman-inspired items to trendy and contemporary designs.

Ceramics:

Hand-painted pottery: The town of Çanakkale, located outside of Bodrum, is famed for its hand-painted pottery. Look for vividly coloured bowls, plates, and vases embellished with classic Turkish themes.

Iznik tiles: These exquisite hand-painted tiles were previously used to adorn Ottoman palaces and mosques. Today, you can purchase replicas of Iznik tiles in Bodrum, ideal for bringing a touch of Ottoman grandeur to your house.

Other Souvenirs:

Leather goods: Bodrum has a booming leather industry, and you'll discover a broad choice of coats, purses, and wallets crafted from high-quality leather.

Spices and herbs: Take home a taste of Bodrum with a range of local spices and herbs, such as saffron, cumin, and oregano.

Olive oil: Bodrum is famed for its olive oil production, so make sure to pick up a bottle of this tasty and nutritious memento.

Traditional Crafts:

Bodrum is home to a variety of ancient crafts that have been handed down through generations. These crafts are not merely a source of revenue for local artists but also a method of maintaining the region's distinct culture and legacy. Some of the most popular traditional crafts in Bodrum include:

Carpet weaving: The art of carpet weaving has a centuries-old history in Bodrum, and there are still a handful of families that make carpets using traditional techniques.

Silverwork: Bodrum's silversmiths are famous for their talent and artistry. You'll discover a wide choice of silver jewellery and other goods, like platters and bowls.

Wood carving: Wood carving is another prominent skill in Bodrum, and you'll find anything from little ornamental pieces to furniture crafted from locally sourced wood.

Where to Buy Souvenirs and Traditional Crafts:

The greatest locations to purchase souvenirs and traditional crafts in Bodrum are the local markets and artisan stores. The Bodrum Bazaar is a terrific place to start, with its labyrinthine lanes packed with booths offering everything from carpets and jewellery to spices and souvenirs. You'll also discover a variety of artisan stores in the town center, where you may purchase straight from the producers.

When shopping for souvenirs and traditional crafts, it's crucial to conduct your homework and be prepared to negotiate. Prices might vary greatly, so it's a good idea to check around before you make a buy. And don't be scared to haggle! Bargaining is a part of life in Turkey, and it's anticipated by both the buyer and the seller.

EMILY CATLETT

CHAPTER 6

DINING AND NIGHTLIFE

LOCAL CUISINE AND RESTAURANTS

Here are some of the must-try local meals in Bodrum:

Meze: A collection of tiny, tapas-style foods, excellent for sharing. Be sure to sample the grilled octopus, dolmas (stuffed grape leaves), and cacık (a yoghurt and cucumber dip).

Giritli Tavuk: Chicken cooked in a creamy yoghurt sauce with garlic and herbs.

Kofte: Grilled meatballs, generally cooked with lamb or beef.

Mantısı: Tiny dumplings filled with meat or veggies, eaten with yoghurt and garlic sauce.

Baklava: A delicious pastry composed of layers of filo dough, almonds, and honey.

Here are some of the greatest restaurants in Bodrum:

Çıngar Meyhane: A typical Turkish restaurant with a magnificent location on the seaside.

Macakizi Restaurant: A family-run restaurant dishing up great home-cooked meals.

Nusr-Et restaurant: If you're looking for a splurge, this upmarket restaurant is the place to go.

Marina Yacht Club: This restaurant provides amazing views of the bay and serves fresh fish.

Mykonos Restaurant: A taste of Greece in Bodrum, this restaurant delivers genuine Greek meals.

BARS AND CLUBS

Bar Street

Bar Street is the hub of Bodrum's nightlife scene. This busy street is dotted with pubs and clubs, each with its own distinct character. From thumping club music to a chilled-out atmosphere, there's something for everyone on Bar Street.

Some of the most popular pubs on Bar Street include:

Havana: This Cuban-themed club is usually filled with people dancing to salsa and Latin music.

Carpe Diem: This rooftop bar provides amazing views of the Bodrum Castle and the Aegean Sea.

Macan: This cocktail bar is an excellent location to have a well-made drink and people-watch.

Beach Clubs

Bodrum is also home to some of the top beach clubs in the world. These upscale locations provide a combination of sunbathing, swimming, eating, and partying. Many beach clubs feature permanent DJs and offer frequent events, making them the ideal spot to spend a day (or night) in style.

Some of the most popular beach clubs in Bodrum include:

Nikki Beach Bodrum: This world-renowned beach club is noted for its lavish environment and famous clients.

Maçakızı: This beach club is situated on a quiet cove and provides spectacular views of the Aegean Sea.

Crystal Bay Beach Club: This family-friendly beach club is a terrific spot to relax and enjoy the sunlight.

Clubs If you're seeking to dance the night away, then Bodrum's clubs are the place to be. These bright establishments remain open till the early hours of the morning and are always crowded with people seeking to have a good time.

Among the most well-liked clubs in Bodrum are:

Halikarnas Disco: This is the biggest disco in Bodrum and is famed for its laser displays and fireworks.

Aura Club: This club is popular with the younger population and is recognized for its electronic music.

Xyst: This club is a little more expensive and is a terrific location to see and be seen.

Suggestions for arranging your night out in Bodrum:

Dress to impress: Bodrum's nightlife scene is magnificent, so dress up to feel your best.

Pace yourself: It's tempting to get caught up in the thrill of Bodrum's nightlife, but don't forget to pace yourself. There's no need to attempt to complete it all in one night.

Stay safe: Bodrum is a fairly safe town, but it's always vital to be aware of your surroundings and take measures. Don't leave your beverages alone, and be wary about taking drinks from strangers.

Have fun! Bodrum's nightlife is all about letting go and having a wonderful time. So relax, dance, and enjoy yourselves!

NIGHTLIFE HOTSPOTS

For the Clubbers:

Halikarnas Disco: No Bodrum nightlife guide would be complete without mentioning Halikarnas, the iconic club that has been throbbing with energy since the 1970s. This mega-club is not simply a place to dance; it's an experience. Prepare to be wowed by pyrotechnics, laser displays, and performances by international DJs.

Aura Club: Aura is another Bodrum institution noted for its open-air location and breathtaking views of the Bodrum Castle. The club features various dance floors, each with its own unique mood, appealing to a varied population.

Macan Beach Club: If you're searching for a club with a coastal backdrop, Macan is the place to go. Dance beneath the stars to the rhythms of international DJs, take a swim in the cool Aegean, or just rest on one of the sumptuous loungers.

For the Chiller:

Gümüslük: This lovely town, situated a short drive from Bodrum, is a sanctuary for those seeking a more calm nightlife experience. Stroll along the harborfront, flanked with traditional meyhanes (taverns), where you may eat delicious seafood and live Greek music.

Yalikavak Marina: The Yalikavak Marina is a stylish and bustling location packed with upmarket clubs and restaurants. Sip on beverages while you watch the yachts bobbing in the port, or have a great lunch overlooking the Aegean.

Bitez: Bitez is a popular family resort, but it also boasts a busy nightlife scene. Head to the main strip for a choice of pubs and restaurants, or see a live music performance at one of the numerous oceanfront cafés.

CHAPTER 7

DAY TRIPS AND EXCURSIONS

GREEK ISLANDS (KOS, RHODES)

Kos:

Kos Overview: Kos, part of the Dodecanese islands, is a lovely resort with a history stretching back to ancient times. Known for its well-preserved ancient monuments, stunning beaches, and dynamic environment, it's a fantastic destination for a day trip or a short adventure.

Activities:

Visit Asklepion:

Start your day with a visit to Asklepion, an ancient healing institution devoted to Asklepios, the deity of healing. Explore the remains and picture the ancient medicinal treatments that took place here.

Explore Kos Town:

Head to Kos Town and explore through its tiny alleys dotted with shops, cafés, and historical sites. Don't miss the historic Castle of the Knights and the majestic Tree of Hippocrates, thought to be the tree beneath which Hippocrates lectured his pupils.

EMILY CATLETT

Relax at Therma Beach:

Unwind at Therma Beach, noted for its natural hot springs. Enjoy a soothing bath in the warm waters while watching the Aegean Sea.

Bike Tour:

Rent a bike and explore the island's gorgeous landscape. Kos is very level, making it a great place for a leisurely bike ride.

Rhodes:

Rhodes Overview: Rhodes, the biggest of the Dodecanese islands, is an intriguing combination of ancient heritage and dynamic contemporary life. The Old Town of Rhodes is a UNESCO World Heritage Site, and the island provides a varied variety of activities.

Activities:

Discover the Old Town:

Begin your adventure in Rhodes by experiencing its historic Old Town. Wander along cobblestone alleyways, explore the Palace of the Grand Master, and marvel at the amazing medieval architecture.

Visit the Acropolis of Rhodes:

Head to the Acropolis of Rhodes to experience ancient remains and magnificent views of the island. The Temple of Apollo is a highlight, displaying the island's historical importance.

EMILY CATLETT

Relax at Lindos Beach:

Take a journey to Lindos, a charming hamlet with a gorgeous acropolis. After seeing the ancient buildings, rest on the neighbouring Lindos Beach with its crystal-clear waves.

Boat Trip to Symi Island:

Extend your journey by taking a boat ride to Symi Island, noted for its beautiful neoclassical buildings. Explore the picturesque waterfront, see the Panormitis Monastery, and savour local food.

Logistics and Tips:

Transportation:

Ferries and catamarans travel regularly between the islands, offering a handy form of Transportation for day visits.

Timing:

Start your day early to make the most of your time on the islands. Many attractions open in the morning and shut in the late afternoon.

Local Cuisine:

Sample the native food, including moussaka, souvlaki, and baklava. Many beachfront tavernas provide fresh fish with a view.

Cultural Sensitivity:

Respect local norms and traditions, particularly while visiting religious places. Dress modestly and stick to any rules stated.

EPHESUS ANCIENT CITY

1. Historical Overview:

Ephesus, built in the 10th century BC, played a significant role in the ancient world. As a large port city, it functioned as a lively centre for commerce, culture, and religious activity. Over the ages, it saw the rise and fall of civilizations, including the Greeks, Romans, and Byzantines, each leaving their unique stamp on the cityscape.

2. Key Attractions:

Celsus Library: An iconic edifice, the Celsus Library is a monument to the intellectual power of ancient Ephesus. Its front, embellished with figures depicting wisdom, morality, knowledge, and heroism, remains a symbol of architectural splendour.

Theatre of Ephesus: This ancient theatre, housing up to 25,000 people, staged plays and gatherings, making it a cultural focus. Its grandeur and acoustics are awe-inspiring, exhibiting the technical wonders of the period.

Temple of Artemis: Once one of the Seven Wonders of the Ancient World, the Temple of Artemis endures as a painful reminder of the city's religious importance. Although just a few columns remain, they create a sense of the temple's previous majesty.

Terrace Houses: Offering a look into the everyday life of Ephesus' wealthy, the Terrace Houses showcase beautiful mosaics, frescoes, and modern heating systems. Visitors may observe the splendour and refinement of ancient Roman life.

3. Planning Your Day Trip:

Start Early: To get the most out of your day, start your trip early in the morning. This offers adequate time to explore the huge archaeological site without feeling hurried.

Guided Tours: Consider hiring a professional guide to discover the historical tales and hidden jewels of Ephesus. Their observations may enrich the whole experience and add perspective to the ruins.

Comfortable Attire and Footwear: Ephesus requires a good bit of walking, so wear comfortable clothes and sturdy shoes. Sun protection, such as helmets and sunscreen, is also advised.

Ancient Ephesus Museum: Extend your historical adventure by visiting the Ephesus Museum, which contains objects and sculptures uncovered during archaeological digs.

4. Culinary Delights: After a day of sightseeing, eat the local cuisine at surrounding restaurants. Turkish sweets, kebabs, and baklava are just a few of the scrumptious alternatives to indulge in, delivering a flavour of the region's gastronomic history.

5. Souvenirs & Mementos: Before finishing your day tour, browse the local marketplaces for souvenirs. Authentic Turkish carpets, pottery, and handcrafted crafts make for wonderful memories, embodying the essence of Ephesus.

PAMUKALLE

1. Understanding Pamukkale:

Pamukkale, meaning "cotton castle" in Turkish, is a UNESCO World Heritage Site noted for its terraces of white carbonate minerals created by gushing hot spring water. The terraces, like cascading pools, form a strange environment that has captivated travellers for ages.

2. Planning Your Day Trip:

a. Departure Points: - Most day excursions to Pamukkale begin from famous tourist destinations like Istanbul, Izmir, and Antalya. - Options include guided excursions, private transfers, or rental automobiles for those preferring a more autonomous experience.

b. Duration: - Day tours normally range from 12-14 hours, giving for enough exploration of Pamukkale's key attractions.

3. Must-Visit Attractions:

a. Hierapolis: - Explore the ancient city of Hierapolis, an archaeological marvel near Pamukkale. - Highlights include the well-preserved theatre, the Necropolis, and the Temple of Apollo.

b. Pamukkale Thermal Pools: - Ascend the terraces barefoot to feel the warm, mineral-rich waters. - Don't miss the chance to get gorgeous images of the pools against the background of the surrounding countryside.

c. Cleopatra's Pool: - Visit the Cleopatra Antique Pool inside Hierapolis, where you may swim amid ancient ruins in mild thermal waters.

4. Practical Tips:

a. Footwear: - Wear comfortable shoes suited for strolling on the travertine terraces.

b. Consider carrying flip-flops to shield your feet from the heated surfaces.

c. Swimwear: - If going to swim in Cleopatra's Pool or the hot pools, bring Swimwear and a towel.

d. Sun Protection: - Given the sunny temperature, apply sunscreen, sunglasses, and a hat to shelter yourself from the sun.

5. Cultural Etiquette:

a. Respect for Heritage: - Adhere to norms that maintain the integrity of the historical sites. - Avoid touching or climbing on old buildings.

b. Environmental Conservation: - Be sensitive to the environment; avoid trash and remain on authorized walkways.

6. Culinary Delights:

a. Local Cuisine: Sample real Turkish meals in the adjacent town of Denizli or inside Pamukkale itself.

Popular selections include kebabs, mezes, and traditional sweets.

DALYAN MUD BATHS

1. Overview of Dalyan:

Geography: Situated along the Dalyan River, Dalyan is recognized for its lush foliage, meandering rivers, and closeness to the Mediterranean Sea.

History: Rich in history, Dalyan is bordered by historical remains, notably the ancient city of Kaunos and the rock-cut Lycian tombs.

2. The Dalyan Mud Baths Experience:

Natural Mud Pools: The mud baths of Dalyan are known for their medicinal powers. Visitors may immerse themselves in natural mud pools, which are considered to provide restorative advantages for the skin.

Mineral-Rich Mud: The mud in Dalyan is rich in minerals, including sulfur and magnesium, which are recognized for their skin-nourishing and detoxifying benefits.

Skin Benefits: The mud is supposed to have exfoliating effects, leaving the skin feeling smooth and refreshed. Many tourists like putting mud all over their bodies for a full-body spa treatment.

3. Day Trip Itinerary:

Morning Exploration: Start the day by touring the historical monuments of Dalyan, such as the ancient city of Kaunos and the Lycian tombs cut into the cliffs.

Boat tour: Embark on a leisurely boat tour down the Dalyan River, soaking in the magnificent views of the surrounding landscape.

Mud Bath Session: Arrive at the mud baths and enjoy a therapeutic mud bath session, applying the mineral-rich mud to your skin.

Hot Springs and Sulphur Pools: After the mud bath, enjoy the neighbouring hot springs and sulphur pools, giving a peaceful and tranquil experience.

4. Health and Wellness Benefits:

Skin renewal: The minerals in the mud are thought to stimulate skin renewal, providing visitors with a rejuvenated and young shine.

Relaxation and Stress Relaxation: The whole experience, from the boat voyage to the mud baths, delivers a feeling of peace and stress relaxation, improving general well-being.

Detoxifying: The mud is supposed to help detoxify, pulling away pollutants from the skin and producing a sensation of cleaning.

5. Practical Tips for Visitors:

Clothes: Wear a swimsuit or comfortable clothes that can be readily washed since the mud might stain.

Sun Protection: Bring sunscreen, a hat, and sunglasses to protect yourself from the sun throughout the boat journey and outdoor activities.

Camera: Don't forget your camera to record the stunning scenery and unforgettable moments throughout the expedition.

EMILY CATLETT

CHAPTER 8

EVENTS AND FESTIVALS

BODRUM INTERNATIONAL BALLET FESTIVALS

About:

The Bodrum International Dance Festival is one of the most famous dance festivals in the world. It is held yearly in Bodrum, Turkey, between July and August. The event was started in 1996 by Arif Erdem, a Turkish businessman and ballet aficionado. The festival comprises performances by world-renowned ballet companies and performers, as well as workshops, masterclasses, and other activities. The event is hosted in the historic amphitheatre of Bodrum Castle, which offers a spectacular background for the performances.

History:

The Bodrum International Ballet Festival was started in 1996 by Arif Erdem, a Turkish businessman and ballet aficionado. Erdem had an ambition of launching a world-class ballet festival in his hometown of Bodrum.

He was inspired by the festivals he had witnessed in Europe, and he felt that Bodrum, with its magnificent environment and rich history, would be the ideal venue for a ballet festival. The inaugural festival was held in 1997, and it was an instant success. Since then, the festival has risen in popularity and significance, and it is currently regarded as one of the most prominent ballet festivals in the world.

Performances: The Bodrum International Ballet Festival showcases performances by world-renowned ballet groups and artists. Some of the groups that have performed at the festival include the Bolshoi Ballet, the Royal Ballet, the Paris Opera Ballet, and the American Ballet Theatre. The event also offers performances from up-and-coming dancers from throughout the globe.

Workshops and masterclasses: In addition to performances, the Bodrum International Ballet Festival also provides workshops and masterclasses for dancers of various abilities. The workshops are offered by professional ballet instructors and choreographers, and they provide dancers with a chance to master new techniques and enhance their technique. The masterclasses are given by globally famous dancers, and they provide dancers an opportunity to learn from the finest in the field.

Other events:

The Bodrum International Ballet Festival also includes a variety of other events, such as cinema screenings, exhibits, and galas. These programs give festival-goers an opportunity to learn more about ballet and explore the culture of Bodrum.

Influence: The Bodrum International Ballet Festival has had a huge influence on the town of Bodrum. The event has attracted worldwide attention to Bodrum, and it has helped to enhance the town's economy. The festival has also made Bodrum a more cultural destination, and it has helped to spread the passion for ballet throughout Turkey.

BODRUM JAZZ FESTIVAL

Location:

Bodrum is a renowned tourist destination noted for its magnificent beaches, crystal blue seas, and historical sites. The village is located on the Bodrum Peninsula, overlooking the Aegean Sea. The festival itself takes place at several locations across the town, including open-air stages, concert halls, and jazz clubs.

Date:

The Bodrum Jazz Festival is normally held in the final week of August, lasting for roughly a week. This time is great for guests as they may enjoy the event during the wonderful late summer weather of Bodrum.

History of the Festival:

The inaugural Bodrum Jazz Festival was held in 2004 and has since become a significant event in the world of jazz music. The festival was first launched with the objective of promoting jazz music and bringing together jazz performers from various regions of the globe. It has now developed into an international event that draws a broad audience and famous jazz musicians from across the globe.

Festival Lineup:

Each year, the Bodrum Jazz Festival presents a broad spectrum of jazz music, including classic, contemporary, and fusion jazz. The event brings together notable worldwide jazz performers as well as brilliant local artists. Some of the noteworthy personalities that have played at the event in the past include Marcus Miller, Didier Lockwood, Avishai Cohen, and Tommy Emmanuel.

Locations:

The event takes place at several locations across Bodrum, delivering an immersive musical experience. The primary stage is the Bodrum Castle, a historical monument that goes back to the 15th century. This majestic castle offers a stunning background for the music performances. Other venues include the open-air Yalıkavak Marina Amphitheater, the D-Marin Turgutreis, and many jazz clubs in the town.

Activities:

Besides the major music concerts, the Bodrum Jazz Festival also incorporates seminars, masterclasses, jam sessions, and street performances. These give festival-goers a chance to connect with the artists, learn more about jazz music, and perhaps join in jam sessions themselves.

BODRUM CUP SAILING REGATTA

History of the Bodrum Cup Sailing Regatta

The Bodrum Cup Sailing Regatta was originally conducted in 1989 by a group of sailing enthusiasts who sought to promote and preserve the traditional Gulet (wooden sailboat) construction and sailing culture in the Bodrum area. This event has expanded enormously over the years and has become one of the most prominent sailing competitions in Turkey, drawing hundreds of sailors and spectators every year.

When and where is the Bodrum Cup Sailing Regatta Held?

The Bodrum Cup Sailing Regatta takes place in the final week of October every year. This is when the weather in Bodrum is great for sailing, with temperatures averaging about 20 degrees Celsius and mild breezes.

The event normally begins at the port of Bodrum and follows a course around the adjacent islands and bays, including pauses for sightseeing and cultural events along the way. The race normally concludes back at the port of Bodrum, where the victors are celebrated with a lavish awards ceremony.

EMILY CATLETT

How to Participate in the Bodrum Cup Sailing Regatta

Participating in the Bodrum Cup Sailing Regatta is not confined to professional sailors exclusively. The event invites all sailing enthusiasts, from expert sailors to novices. To participate, you may either bring your own boat or hire one from local firms. However, to join the race, your boat must match specific requirements, including length, design, and safety restrictions. Teams may consist of up to eight individuals, and there is a registration fee for participation in the tournament.

What to Expect at the Bodrum Cup Sailing Regatta?

The Bodrum Cup Sailing Regatta is not only about the race; it's also a week-long celebration of sailing and Bodrum's distinctive culture. Throughout the week, there are different activities and events scheduled for participants and spectators, including cultural performances, open-air concerts, food bazaars, and more. The race itself is separated into numerous categories, including professional, amateur, and traditional Gulet boats, giving a unique and entertaining experience for everyone participating.

CHAPTER 9

PRACTICAL INFORMATION

WEATHER AND BEST TIME TO VISIT

Weather in Bodrum:

Bodrum has a Mediterranean climate, typified by hot and dry summers and warm and rainy winters. The weather in Bodrum is influenced by the Mediterranean Sea; therefore, the temperature stays mild throughout the year. The summer months run from June to September, with July and August being the warmest and busiest months. The average temperature during these months varies from 26-34 degrees Celsius, making it excellent for aquatic sports and beach vacations.

The winter months in Bodrum occur from December to February, with temperatures decreasing to an average of 6-11 degrees Celsius. The weather during this season is temperate and pleasant, giving it an excellent opportunity to visit the historical and cultural attractions of Bodrum without the crowds. However, be prepared for intermittent showers throughout this season.

Best Time to Visit Bodrum:

The optimum time to visit Bodrum is from mid-April to mid-June and from September to October. This time is called the shoulder season, and the weather is moderate and pleasant, making it great for outdoor activities and sightseeing. The tourist population is generally considerably smaller during this season, and you may get fantastic prices on lodgings and airfare.

If you are a beach lover, then the summer months of July and August are the finest time to visit Bodrum. These months provide great beach weather, and you may enjoy numerous water sports and activities. However, it is advisable to schedule your vacation in early July or late August to avoid the peak season crowds and exorbitant rates.

If you want to enjoy the exciting nightlife of Bodrum, then the summer months are the best time to go. Bodrum has a reputation for its bustling pubs, clubs, and beach parties, which are in full swing throughout the summer season. You may also visit the legendary Halikarnas Nights, a stunning open-air nightclub that offers worldwide DJs and live music acts.

Things to Keep in Mind:

While planning your vacation to Bodrum, bear in mind that it is a famous tourist destination, and the peak season may become busy and pricey. It is advisable to book your hotels and flights in advance to prevent any last-minute stress. Also, be sure to pack sunscreen, sunglasses, and a hat during the summer months since the sun may be extremely powerful.

In case you intend to travel during the winter months, be sure to take warm clothing and a raincoat to prepare for possible downpours. Some of the tourist sites and aquatic activities may also be closed during this period, so it is wise to check ahead.

LOCAL CUSTOMS AND ETIQUETTE

Greetings:

A handshake and a warm grin are the most popular welcomes in Bodrum.

When greeting someone older or of better social status, it is traditional to bow slightly and say "Merhaba" (pronounced mer-ha-ba).

Close friends and relatives may hug or kiss one another on the cheek.

Dress Code:

Bodrum is a rather laid-back town, although it's always wise to err on the side of modesty while dressed.

Avoid too exposing apparel, particularly in religious or conservative communities.

When attending mosques, you are required to cover your shoulders and knees, and women should cover their heads.

Dining Etiquette:

Meals are a social event in Turkey, so be prepared to linger and enjoy the discussion.

It is usual to wait for the oldest person at the table to start eating before diving in.

Bread is offered with most meals and is considered a tool. Use it to scoop up food or soak up sauces.

Tipping is not required in Turkey; however, if you wish to express your thanks, a tiny round-up of the amount is sufficient.

Gift-Giving:

If you are welcomed to a Turkish house, it is usual to offer a little gift, such as flowers, candy, or a bottle of wine.

Gifts are not opened immediately, so don't be shocked if your host lays it away till later.

Other Customs:

Smoking is popular in Turkey, but be aware of where you light up. Smoking is not banned in most public locations, including restaurants and public transit.

Haggling is typical in marketplaces and bazaars. Don't be afraid to haggle for a fair deal, but always do it in a courteous and respectful manner.

Be prepared to be patient. Things don't always run on schedule in Turkey, so relax and enjoy the laid-back pace of life.

SAFETY TIPS

General Safety:

Stay informed: Keep tabs on local news and alerts. Register with your embassy for updates and help.

Be vigilant: Petty theft may occur, particularly in busy settings. Keep an eye on your stuff and avoid exhibiting valuables publicly.

Respect local customs: Dress modestly while visiting religious places or conservative regions. Public expressions of love are often frowned upon.

Beware of scams: Be careful with unsolicited offers, particularly for tours or taxis. Stick to reliable companies and discuss pricing ahead.

Traffic: Taxis are numerous, but negotiate prices before getting in. Roads may be crowded, particularly during peak season.

Sun safety: Bodrum's sun is powerful. Use sunscreen, wear protective clothes, and remain hydrated, particularly around noon.

EMILY CATLETT

Beach Safety:

Lifeguards: Check whether your selected beach has lifeguards and swim within specified zones.

Rip currents: Be wary of rip currents, particularly at specific beaches. Heed lifeguards' cautions and don't panic if trapped in one. Swim parallel to the coast to escape.

Water sports: Choose reliable providers for water activities like paragliding or jet skiing. Ensure sufficient safety equipment is given.

Marine life: Be aware of jellyfish, particularly during specific seasons. Wear protective gear if required.

Nightlife Safety:

Stick to well-lighted areas: Avoid poorly lit streets and lanes, particularly at night.

Beware of drugged beverages: Never take drinks from strangers. Keep an eye on your drinks, and don't leave them unattended.

Transportation: Arrange trustworthy Transportation ahead, particularly if returning late at night. Avoid using cabs alone whenever feasible.

Stay alert of your surroundings: Be careful of your things and surroundings, especially in apparently secure settings.

USEFUL PHRASES

Greetings and Politeness:

Merhaba (pronounced mare-hah-bah): Hello (the most common greeting)

Günaydın (pronounced goon-eye-din): Good morning

İyi günler (pronounced ee-yee goo-n-ler): Good day (used on meeting or parting)

İyi akşamlar (pronounced ee-yee ak-sham-lar): Good evening

Nasılsınız? (pronounced nah-suh-sunuz): How are you? (formal)

İyiyim, teşekkür ederim (pronounced ee-yee-yim, teshekkur ederim): I'm fine, thank you

Lütfen (pronounced luht-fen): Please

Teşekkür ederim (pronounced teshekkur ederim): Thank you

Rica ederim (pronounced ree-jah ederim): You're welcome

Basic Communication:

Evet (pronounced ay-vet): Yes

Hayır (pronounced hah-yir): No

Anlamıyorum (pronounced an-lah-mih-yorum): I don't understand

Konuşabilir miyim? (pronounced konu-shah-bi-li-rim mi?)Can I speak (with you)?

İngilizce konuşuyor musunuz? (pronounced ingilizje konusuyor musunuz)Do you speak English?

Biraz Türkçe biliyorum (pronounced bi-raz turkce bi-li-yorum): I know a little Turkish

Numbers and Shopping:

Bir (pronounced bir): One

İki (pronounced ee-ki): Two

Üç (pronounced uch): Three

Dört (pronounced dort): Four

*Beş (pronounced besh): Five

Ne kadar? (pronounced neh ka-dar)How much?

Pahalı (pronounced pah-hah-lu): Expensive

Ucuz (pronounced oo-jooz): Cheap

Bunu alabilir miyim? (pronounced bunu ah-lah-bi-li-yim mi?)Can I have this?

EMILY CATLETT

Directions and Transportation:

Nerede? (pronounced neh-reh-deh): Where is...?

Tuvalet nerede? (pronounced tuvalet neh-reh-deh)Where is the toilet?

Otobüs durağı nerede? (pronounced otobus durağı neh-reh-deh)Where is the bus stop?

Taksi (pronounced tak-si): Taxi

Durak (pronounced doo-rak): Stop

Useful Tips:

Pronunciation is key! Listen to native speakers, and don't be afraid to try.

Gestures can be helpful for emphasis.

A smile and a polite tone go a long way.

Don't be discouraged if you make mistakes - everyone does!

Learning a few basic phrases will show respect and effort to the locals, enhancing your travel experience.

EMILY CATLETT

96 BODRUM TRAVEL GUIDE 2024

CONCLUSION

As we wave goodbye to the pages of our Bodrum Travel Guide 2024, it's my honest hope that this literary trip has been as stimulating for you as it has been for me. From the sun-kissed beaches to the labyrinthine alleyways steeped in history, Bodrum uncovers itself as a treasure trove ready to be discovered.

Our guide has precisely chosen the essence of Bodrum, unravelling its unique fabric of culture, history, and natural beauty. We've walked through the ancient marvels of the Mausoleum at Halicarnassus, dipped our toes in the crystal-clear waters of the Aegean Sea, and drank delicious Turkish tea while soaking in the warmth of local hospitality.

But beneath the colourful descriptions and practical suggestions is the pulse of Bodrum, a location that exceeds the bounds of a traditional tourist experience. It's a location where blue sky meets turquoise oceans, where the whispers of history reverberate through old ruins, and where the vivid energy of the bazaars beckons you to immerse yourself in a world of colours, fragrances, and tastes.

As you reflect on the chapters of this book, visualize the moments that await you—the stunning sunsets above Bodrum Castle, the laughter-filled nights in coastal tavernas, and the calm found in the quiet nooks of Bodrum's hidden jewels. This book is more than words on paper; it's an invitation to build your own Bodrum tale, one that will stay in your memory long after your return home.

Now, when the last page turns, consider this your call to action. Bodrum beckons and the events recounted in these pages are simply glimpses of what awaits you. Whether you're a history aficionado, a sun-seeker, or a connoisseur of gastronomic pleasures, Bodrum has plenty to offer.

Pack your luggage, let the sea air lead you, and let the old stones speak their stories. Your experience in Bodrum is filled with exploration, relaxation, and the type of moments that make a vacation into a lasting memory.

So, dear reader, the issue is not if you should visit Bodrum; it's when. The moment is now, the destination is Bodrum, and the experience is yours to grab. Embark on this voyage, and let Bodrum etch itself into the fabric of your most treasured travel memories.

Printed in Great Britain
by Amazon